101

FACTS ABOUT

LIONEL MESSI

Essential Trivia, Quotes, and Questions for Super Fans

FALCON FOCUS

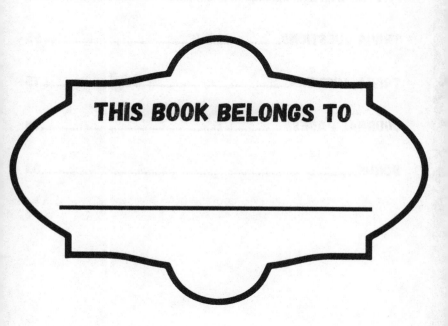

THIS BOOK BELONGS TO

_____

TABLE OF CONTENTS

INTRODUCTION

Welcome to *101 Fascinating Facts About Lionel Messi,* a comprehensive journey through the life and career of Lionel Messi, one of the most iconic figures in the world of football. This book is a tribute to the sheer brilliance and unparalleled achievements of a player who has not only rewritten the record books but has also captured the hearts of millions around the globe.

As you delve into these pages, you will discover a curated collection of facts, anecdotes, and milestones that chronicle Messi's journey from a young prodigy at Rosario to a global superstar. Each fact has been meticulously researched and presented to offer a complete picture of Messi's extraordinary influence both on and off the pitch.

It is important to note that the statistics and numbers mentioned in this book are based on records and achievements as of October 2023. Lionel Messi, a living legend still active in the sport, continues to play at the highest level. Consequently, the numbers and records associated with his name are subject to change as he continues to add to his remarkable legacy.

DID YOU KNOW?

Messi's full name is Lionel Andrés Messi Cuccitini. He was born on June 24, 1987, in Rosario, Argentina. He grew up in a football-loving family in a city that's also the birthplace of other famous Argentinian footballers like Ángel Di María.

Lionel's father, Jorge Messi, was deeply involved in his son's football journey. As a local steel factory manager, he balanced work with coaching Lionel and his brothers in their early football endeavors.

DID YOU KNOW?

Celia Cuccittini, Lionel's mother, played a pivotal nurturing role. While working part-time as a cleaner, she provided strong emotional support and encouragement, vital in Lionel's development as a person and an athlete.

Lionel Messi, the third of four children, has a significant age gap with his siblings. Born in 1979, Rodrigo is eight years his senior and manages Lionel's professional schedule. Matías, born in 1982, five years older, oversees his charitable foundation. María Sol, his younger sister, born in 1993, six years his junior, maintains a private life but shares a close bond with Lionel.

DID YOU KNOW?

Lionel Messi started playing soccer at a young age, around 4 years old. He joined a local club, Grandoli, where his father coached him.

At age 8, Lionel Messi joined Newell's Old Boys, a prominent football club in his hometown, Rosario, where his exceptional talent quickly set him apart as a prodigious young player in the football world.

DID YOU KNOW?

Lionel Messi was diagnosed with idiopathic short stature, a type of growth hormone deficiency, around the age of 10. This condition hindered his growth and physical development, making him noticeably smaller and shorter than his peers. His treatment involved regular injections of growth hormones to help normalize his growth.

Facing financial challenges, Lionel Messi's family approached River Plate, a prominent Argentinian football club, for assistance with his costly growth hormone treatments. Despite River Plate's interest in Messi's talent, they could not fund his medical needs either.

DID YOU KNOW?

In 2000, at the age of 13, Lionel Messi moved to Barcelona, Spain, with his family after FC Barcelona offered to pay for his medical treatments for growth hormone deficiency and included him in their youth academy, La Masia.

His initial contract with FC Barcelona was famously signed on a paper napkin. This unconventional agreement, by FC Barcelona's technical secretary Carles Rexach, symbolized the club's immediate and decisive commitment to Messi's extraordinary talent.

DID YOU KNOW?

In February 2002, after joining Barcelona's youth academy, La Masia, at age 13, Lionel Messi was officially enrolled in the Royal Spanish Football Federation (RFEF). This formal registration marked a significant step in his journey, legitimizing his status as a player within the Spanish football system and paving the way for his professional career.

———————————————

Messi signed his first official contract with FC Barcelona in June 2004. This contract solidified his status as a professional player with the club.

WHAT IS LA LIGA?

La Liga, officially known as La Liga Santander for sponsorship reasons, is the top professional football division of the Spanish football league system. Administered by the Liga Nacional de Fútbol Profesional, it is one of the premier football leagues in the world, and has been in existence since its formation in 1929.

Consisting of 20 teams, La Liga operates on a system of promotion and relegation with the Segunda División. The season runs from August to May, with each club playing a total of 38 matches (19 at home and 19 away). Teams receive three points for a win, one point for a draw, and no points for a loss, with the rankings determined by total points accumulated.

La Liga has gained a reputation for being one of the best football leagues globally due to its high-quality and technically skilled gameplay. It is particularly known for producing world-class footballers and is home to some of the most successful and popular football clubs in the world, such as Real Madrid, Barcelona, and Atlético Madrid.

La Liga was the first national league to be broadcast in Europe and has since become one of the most widely followed and televised sporting leagues in the world. The league's popularity is bolstered by its high-profile talents, competitive matches, and tactical innovation, making it a significant contributor to the global football industry.

DID YOU KNOW?

Lionel officially appeared for FC Barcelona's first team on October 16, 2004, in a La Liga match against Espanyol. Entering the game in the 82nd minute, the 17-year-old Messi marked his debut in professional football.

Lionel Messi scored his first official goal for FC Barcelona on May 1, 2005, in a La Liga match against Albacete Balompié. Coming off the bench, Messi found the net with a skillful lob over the goalkeeper, assisted by Ronaldinho.

DID YOU KNOW?

Messi won his first La Liga trophy with FC Barcelona in the 2004/05 season. During that season, he made 7 appearances, all as a substitute, and scored 1 goal.

In 2005, Lionel Messi distinguished himself at the FIFA World Youth Championship by winning both the Golden Ball, awarded to the tournament's best player, and the Golden Shoe, for being the top scorer with 6 goals.

WHAT IS THE UEFA CHAMPIONS LEAGUE?

The UEFA Champions League, often referred to as simply the Champions League, is the most prestigious club competition in European football. Organized by the Union of European Football Associations (UEFA), the tournament has been a cornerstone of European club football since its inception in 1955, originally known as the European Champion Clubs' Cup or simply the European Cup.

The competition involves the top club teams from Europe's most competitive national leagues. Its format has evolved over the years and currently features several stages, including qualifying rounds, a group stage, and knockout rounds culminating in the final. The group stage pits teams in groups of four, with the top two teams from each group advancing to the knockout phase.

The Champions League is celebrated for showcasing high-level football and features many of the world's most renowned clubs like Real Madrid, Barcelona, Manchester United, Bayern Munich, and Juventus. Winning the Champions League is considered one of the highest honors in club football, symbolizing continental supremacy.

The tournament has become known for its iconic anthem, based on George Frideric Handel's Zadok the Priest, which plays before each game. The anthem and the Champions League logo have become symbols of the high quality and prestige associated with European club football's elite competition.

DID YOU KNOW?

Lionel Messi's journey with the Argentine national team began in 2005 with his debut in a friendly against Hungary, where he was notably sent off just one minute after entering the field, sparking debates about the red card's fairness. He scored his first international goal in his sixth appearance for Argentina during a friendly match against Croatia on March 1, 2006.

Lionel scored his first UEFA Champions League goal against Panathinaikos on November 2, 2005. He became the youngest player to score a hat-trick in the tournament at 19, showcasing his talent in a match against Real Madrid in March 2007.

WHAT IS EL CLÁSICO MATCH?

"El Clásico" refers to the football matches between two of the most prominent and successful clubs in Spanish football: FC Barcelona and Real Madrid. The term "El Clásico" translates to "The Classic" in English, emphasizing the historical and intense rivalry between these two clubs.

The matches between Barcelona and Real Madrid are highly anticipated and widely watched, not only in Spain but also around the world. The rivalry is not only based on sporting competition but also has cultural and political dimensions, reflecting the historical tensions between Catalonia (where Barcelona is located) and the rest of Spain, particularly Madrid.

These matches are known for their high level of competition, skillful play, and often intense and dramatic moments. El Clásico is a fixture that captures the attention of football fans globally and is considered one of the biggest and most-watched football rivalries in the world.

El Clásico's global influence is apparent as millions worldwide tune in, transcending language barriers and time zones. The matches showcase football's universal appeal, captivating audiences with skill, strategy, and raw emotion. As the world collectively engages in El Clásico, this rivalry's significance reaches beyond sports, becoming a shared experience that unites diverse cultures in a common passion for football.

DID YOU KNOW?

In the 2005-2006 season, at 18, Messi won his first Champions League trophy with FC Barcelona. He contributed 1 goal and 1 assist in 6 appearances. Still, he missed the final against Arsenal due to injury in a campaign that ended with Barcelona securing the title.

On March 10, 2007, in an El Clásico match against Real Madrid, Lionel Messi scored his first career hat-trick, resulting in a 3-3 draw. This performance made Messi the first player since Iván Zamorano (who did so for Real Madrid in the 1994-95 season) to score a hat-trick in an El Clásico match. This feat was particularly notable as Messi was only 19 years old at the time.

WHAT IS THE COPA DEL REY?

The Copa del Rey (Spanish for "King's Cup") is an annual knockout football competition in Spanish football, organized by the Royal Spanish Football Federation. It was first held in 1903, making it one of the oldest football competitions in the world. The cup is contested by teams from various levels of the Spanish football league system, showcasing a wide range of talent and competition.

The format of the Copa del Rey involves a series of knockout rounds, traditionally starting with single-leg matches in the early rounds, progressing to two-legged ties in the later stages, and culminating in a single-match final. This structure allows for exciting and unpredictable matches, often leading to unexpected outcomes and thrilling moments in Spanish football.

Initially, the competition was mainly contested by teams from the top divisions, but it has since expanded to include teams from lower divisions, giving smaller clubs a chance to compete against the giants of Spanish football. This inclusion adds a unique charm to the tournament, as it allows for classic "David vs. Goliath" matchups.

The winner of the Copa del Rey is awarded a prestigious trophy and often earns a place in the UEFA Europa League for the following season, unless they have already qualified for the UEFA Champions League through their league position. This provides an additional incentive for clubs to perform well in the competition.

DID YOU KNOW?

On April 18, 2007, in a Copa del Rey semi-final match against Getafe, Lionel Messi scored a goal often regarded as one of the best in football history and has been celebrated by many Barcelona fans as the best in the club's history. Messi started with the ball near the halfway line on the right side, sprinted about 197 feet (60 meters), evaded five defenders, and then scored with an angled finish.

In the 2008-2009 season, Lionel Messi was instrumental in FC Barcelona's first-ever treble, winning La Liga, Copa del Rey, and the UEFA Champions League. Messi's standout performances, including being the top scorer in the Champions League, solidified his status as one of the world's premier footballers.

WHAT IS THE BALLON D'OR?

The Ballon d'Or (French for "Golden Ball") is an annual football award presented by France Football. It has been awarded since 1956, although between 2010 and 2015 it was merged with the FIFA World Player of the Year award and known as the FIFA Ballon d'Or. However, in 2016, the Ballon d'Or again became a separate award.

The award is given to the best male footballer in the world for the year, as judged by a panel of international journalists. Each journalist selects the top five players, and points are allocated based on their ranking – the first receiving five points, the second four points, and so on.

Historically, the Ballon d'Or was restricted to European players playing in European clubs. However, this rule was changed in 1995, allowing non-European players to be eligible for the award as long as they were playing for a European club. In 2007, the award was opened to players of any nationality, regardless of the continent in which they played.

The Ballon d'Or is one of the most prestigious individual awards in football and is widely regarded as a symbol of excellence in the sport.

DID YOU KNOW?

On August 23, 2008, Messi played a crucial role in Argentina's Olympic gold medal victory at the Beijing Games. In the final against Nigeria at the Bird's Nest stadium, watched by over 89,000 fans, Messi provided an assist in the 1-0 win. This victory marked Argentina's consecutive Olympic football titles, following their win in 2004, making them the first team to achieve back-to-back Olympic golds in football since Uruguay in 1924 and 1928.

Lionel Messi won his first Ballon d'Or in 2009 at age 22, recognizing him as the world's best player following his pivotal role in FC Barcelona's historic treble-winning season.

DID YOU KNOW?

2010 Lionel Messi retained the Ballon d'Or, winning it for the second consecutive year. His consistent high-level performances throughout the year for both FC Barcelona and the Argentine national team were crucial in earning him this honor again.

In 2011, Messi achieved a remarkable feat by winning the Ballon d'Or for the third consecutive year. His exceptional performances, including key contributions to FC Barcelona's Champions League victory and La Liga triumph.

DID YOU KNOW?

On March 7, 2012, Messi achieved an unprecedented feat in the UEFA Champions League, scoring five goals in a single match against Bayer Leverkusen. This remarkable performance made him the first player in the competition's history to score five goals in a single game. At that time, no one had achieved such a remarkable milestone in the Champions League.

In the 2011-2012 season, Messi continued to break records and collect individual awards. He scored an astounding 73 goals for Barcelona across all competitions, breaking Gerd Muller's longstanding record for the most goals in a calendar year. This remarkable achievement earned him his fourth consecutive Ballon d'Or award, cementing his status as one of the greatest footballers of all time.

WHAT IS THE FIFA WORLD CUP?

The FIFA Club World Cup is an international men's association football competition organized by the Fédération Internationale de Football Association (FIFA), the sport's global governing body. Inaugurated in 2000, the tournament was initially held annually, then biennially, and again annually since 2005. It features the champion clubs from each of the six continental confederations, along with the national league champion from the host country.

The competition is structured as a small tournament with a few rounds, leading to a final that determines the world's top club team. The format typically includes a preliminary round, a quarter-final round, semi-finals, and the final. This format ensures that teams from different continents have the opportunity to compete against each other, making it a true test of global club supremacy.

Initially, the tournament faced challenges in establishing its significance in the football calendar, given the already packed schedule of top teams. However, over time, it has grown in prestige and is now highly coveted by participating clubs. Winning the FIFA Club World Cup is considered a great honor, symbolizing global dominance in club football.

The competition has seen representation from a wide array of clubs, showcasing diverse playing styles and football cultures. Traditionally, teams from Europe and South America have been more successful, reflecting the strength of football in these regions.

DID YOU KNOW?

On March 20, 2012, Messi achieved yet another historic milestone in his career when he became Barcelona's all-time top scorer. At just 24, Messi surpassed the 57-year-old record held by Cesar Rodriguez by scoring a hat-trick against Granada, bringing his total to 234 goals for the club.

In the 2014 FIFA World Cup held in Brazil, Messi played a crucial role for Argentina's national team. He led his country to the World Cup final, scoring four goals in the tournament and providing numerous assists. Although Argentina ultimately finished as runners-up, Messi's performances earned him the Golden Ball award.

DID YOU KNOW?

On November 22, 2014, Messi etched his name even deeper into football history by becoming the all-time top scorer in La Liga. During a match against Sevilla, Messi scored a mesmerizing hat-trick, surpassing the 59-year-old record held by Telmo Zarra with 252 goals in La Liga.

On April 23, 2017, Lionel Messi achieved a historic milestone by scoring his 500th goal for Barcelona in all competitions. He accomplished this feat during a thrilling El Clásico match against Real Madrid at the Santiago Bernabéu stadium. In a highly intense and dramatic match, Messi scored twice, with his 500th goal coming in overtime, securing a crucial 3-2 victory for Barcelona.

WHAT IS THE COPA AMÉRICA?

Established in 1916, the Copa América is the world's oldest international football tournament, exclusively featuring South American national teams and organized by the South American Football Confederation (CONMEBOL). Traditionally held every four years, the competition follows a format of group stages and knockout rounds culminating in a prestigious final. It is renowned for encapsulating the passion and intensity associated with South American football, fostering historic rivalries and delivering matches filled with flair and skill.

Success in the Copa América is highly coveted, second only to the FIFA World Cup, attracting legendary players and showcasing top-tier football talent. Throughout its history, the tournament has evolved, occasionally inviting guest teams from outside the region, broadening its global appeal.

Recent expansions, exemplified by the Copa América Centenario in 2016 and Copa América 2021, sought to enhance competitiveness by including teams from North and Central America, as well as Asia. Despite variations in frequency and structure, the Copa América remains a symbol of football tradition, providing South American nations with a platform to exhibit their prowess on the international stage while preserving the continent's rich footballing heritage.

DID YOU KNOW?

In the 2015 Copa América, Messi led the Argentina national team to the final. However, despite his outstanding performances throughout the tournament, Argentina faced a heartbreaking defeat in the final match against Chile. The final ended in a 0-0 draw, and Chile emerged victorious 4-1 on penalties. Messi scored Argentina's only penalty in the shootout, while Gonzalo Higuain and Ever Banega missed their spot-kicks. Despite the disappointment of losing the final, Messi's exceptional contributions earned him the Player of the Tournament award, with 1 goal and 3 assists.

DID YOU KNOW?

In December 2019, Lionel Messi made history by winning the Ballon d'Or for the sixth time, setting a new record in the competition's history. He outperformed top contenders like Virgil van Dijk and Cristiano Ronaldo to claim the prestigious individual football trophy once again. Messi's remarkable season included scoring 50 goals and providing 18 assists in 59 games.

On December 22, 2020, Lionel Messi achieved yet another historic milestone when he became the top goalscorer with a single club. He surpassed the longstanding record held by Brazilian legend Pelé, who had scored 643 goals with Santos in his native Brazil. Messi achieved this feat by scoring his 644th goal in all competitions for Barcelona during a 0-3 victory over Real Valladolid. Pelé's record had stood for 46 years until Messi's remarkable achievement.

DID YOU KNOW?

In July 2021, Lionel Messi achieved a lifelong dream by leading the Argentina national team to victory in the Copa América. Argentina defeated Brazil 1-0 in the final, securing their first Copa América title in 28 years and Messi's first major international trophy. Messi's contributions were instrumental throughout the tournament, and he was named the Player of the Tournament. He also shared the Golden Boot as the top goalscorer with 4 goals, alongside Luis Díaz, and led in assists with 5.

DID YOU KNOW?

In August 2021, Lionel Messi embarked on a new chapter in his illustrious career by completing a highly anticipated transfer to the French club Paris Saint-Germain (PSG). This move came after Messi's 21-year association with Barcelona, which he joined at 13 and won 35 trophies. His transfer to PSG occurred following the expiration of his contract at Barcelona. Messi made a poignant choice by selecting squad number 30 at PSG, which held sentimental value as it was the number he wore on his Barcelona debut in 2003.

DID YOU KNOW?

In his debut season with Paris Saint-Germain (PSG) during the 2021-2022 campaign, Messi continued to showcase his extraordinary talents. He formed a formidable attacking trio with Neymar and Kylian Mbappé, helping PSG secure the Ligue 1 title.

On November 29, 2021, Lionel Messi added to his already illustrious collection of individual awards by winning his seventh Ballon d'Or.

DID YOU KNOW?

In the 2022 Finalissima held at Wembley Stadium, Lionel Messi once again demonstrated his brilliance on the international stage. Argentina faced Italy in this high-stakes match, which pitted the European championship winner against the Copa América winner. Messi played a pivotal role in Argentina's 3-0 victory, contributing with two assists and earning the Player of the Match title.

DID YOU KNOW?

In the 2022 FIFA World Cup final, held at Lusail Stadium, Lionel Messi added to his legendary career by making a record 26th World Cup finals appearance. In a thrilling and closely contested final, Messi scored Argentina's opening goal with a penalty. However, France's Kylian Mbappé quickly responded with two goals, jeopardizing Argentina's lead. Messi showed his resilience by scoring again in extra-time to restore Argentina's lead, only for Mbappé to level the score once more. With the match tied 3-3 after extra time, it came down to a penalty shootout. Messi once again displayed his composure and skill by scoring Argentina's first goal in the shootout. Argentina eventually won 4-2 in the penalty shootout, ending the nation's 36-year wait for the FIFA World Cup trophy. Messi's exceptional performances throughout the tournament, where he scored 7 goals and provided 3 assists, earned him the Golden Ball as the tournament's best player.

DID YOU KNOW?

In the latter part of his illustrious career, Lionel Messi made a significant move by signing with Major League Soccer (MLS) club Inter Miami. After leaving Paris Saint-Germain (PSG) as a free agent, Messi embarked on a new chapter in his football journey. He signed a two-and-a-half-season contract with Inter Miami, which included an option to extend for a further year, potentially keeping him with the club until the 2026 season.

Antonela Roccuzzo and Lionel Messi, both from Rosario, Argentina, first crossed paths as children and grew up together. They began dating during their teenage years and maintained their relationship for over a decade before getting married in 2017.

DID YOU KNOW?

Lionel Messi and Antonela Roccuzzo's 2017 wedding in Rosario, Argentina, was a star-studded affair. It featured numerous celebrities and footballers, including Messi's Barcelona teammates Gerard Piqué and Luis Suárez and fellow football stars Sergio Agüero and Neymar.

Lionel Messi and Antonela Roccuzzo have three sons: Thiago (2012), Mateo (2015), and Ciro (2018). Messi's social media shares heartwarming family moments, offering glimpses into his life as a devoted family man alongside his football stardom. Notably, the boys show an early interest in soccer, sparking anticipation about whether they may inherit their father's talents on the field.

DID YOU KNOW?

Barcelona served as a second home for Lionel Messi and his family during his iconic tenure with FC Barcelona. While Messi's professional journey took him to various cities, they established deep roots in the Catalan capital. Beyond football, his wife and children embraced the culture, education, and warmth of the city.

Messi's charitable work extends to healthcare, where he has supported the development of medical facilities and initiatives to improve the well-being of children facing health challenges.

DID YOU KNOW?

He founded the Leo Messi Foundation, a philanthropic organization dedicated to improving the lives of disadvantaged children. The foundation focuses on healthcare initiatives, aiming to provide better opportunities and a brighter future for children in need. Through his foundation, Messi has funded educational programs and projects, including the construction of schools and the provision of educational resources. These efforts aim to empower children with quality education and help them break the cycle of poverty.

DID YOU KNOW?

Beyond the foundation, Messi has been actively involved in various charitable activities and donations throughout his career. He has contributed to disaster relief efforts, hospitals, and other causes that align with his commitment to making a positive impact on society. Messi's philanthropic efforts have a global reach, demonstrating his commitment to making a difference in communities worldwide, not limited to his home country of Argentina. His dedication to charitable work has earned him numerous humanitarian awards, underscoring his role as a positive influence both on and off the football field.

DID YOU KNOW?

Messi's star power extends beyond the football pitch. He has endorsed many global brands, including sportswear giant Adidas, soft drink company Pepsi, and technology giant Huawei. These endorsements have not only bolstered his income but have also solidified his status as a marketable icon.

_____

Beyond endorsements, Messi ventured into the fashion industry by launching his own fashion brand, "The Messi Store." This brand offers a clothing and apparel line reflecting Messi's style and taste.

DID YOU KNOW?

Lionel Messi and his family own the "Bellavista del Jardín del Norte" restaurant chain in Argentina.

Bellavista del Jardín del Norte is renowned for its delightful ambiance and diverse menu, offering a taste of Argentine culinary traditions. These establishments have attracted both local patrons and international visitors, contributing to Messi's diversification beyond football while highlighting his dedication to Argentine cuisine.

DID YOU KNOW?

Messi's partnership with the Majestic Hotel Group led to the creation of the opulent "Majestic Messi" hotel in Barcelona.

"Majestic Messi" hotel, strategically located in Barcelona's heart, attracts tourists seeking cultural experiences and iconic landmarks. With an emphasis on exclusivity, elegance, and premium service, it caters to discerning guests. This venture contributes significantly to Barcelona's tourism industry and local economy.

DID YOU KNOW?

Lionel Messi's art collection boasts diverse works, including renowned Catalan surrealist Joan Miró pieces. These artworks are known for their abstract and playful nature, offering a glimpse into Messi's appreciation for imaginative and emotionally evocative creations that transcend the boundaries of reality.

Messi's collaboration with architect Luis Galliussi resulted in "The Messi Collection," a unique furniture line. This venture highlights Messi's passion for interior design, offering meticulously designed pieces that blend aesthetics, functionality, and comfort. "The Messi Collection" allows fans and homeowners to incorporate Messi's distinctive style into their living spaces.

DID YOU KNOW?

Throughout his illustrious career, Lionel Messi has netted an impressive total of 57 hat-tricks.

_____

He holds the record for the fastest hat-trick in La Liga history, scoring three goals in just 12 minutes during a match against Rayo Vallecano.

DID YOU KNOW?

Messi has converted an impressive total of 65 free-kick goals.

_____

He has scored goals in every minute of a football match, from the first to the last.

DID YOU KNOW?

In football, height varies, but talent knows no bounds. Lionel Messi, at 5 feet 7 inches (1.70 meters), and Diego Maradona, at 5 feet 5 inches (1.65 meters), are revered for their excellence. Meanwhile, Marcin Garuch, standing at just 5 feet (1.53 cm), holds the title of the shortest professional soccer player ever.

He has netted 23 goals using his head, showcasing his versatility as a goal scorer.

DID YOU KNOW?

Messi's ambidexterity is a testament to his exceptional footballing talent. While he is famously left-footed, Messi has still netted a substantial 75 goals with his right foot, showcasing his ability to adapt and excel in various situations on the field.

He has been clinical from the penalty spot, converting 77 penalties for Barcelona.

DID YOU KNOW?

Messi has found the back of the net from various positions on the field, with 215 goals coming from the left field, 215 from the right field, and 104 from the center field.

_____

A significant portion of his goals, 385 to be precise, were scored from within the 6-yard box, showcasing his ability to capitalize on close-range opportunities.

DID YOU KNOW?

While he is known for his close-range goals, Messi has also scored from beyond the 18-yard box, with 24 goals from that range.

Messi has not only been a prolific scorer but also a generous provider, recording 205 assists during his time at Barcelona.

DID YOU KNOW?

Messi's remarkable football journey has seen him finish in the top three of the Ballon d'Or voting an astonishing 13 times, securing the runner-up position in 2008, 2013, and 2014. His unparalleled dominance is further exemplified by his record-breaking eight Ballon d'Or wins (Christiano Ronaldo has five), solidifying his legacy as the most decorated recipient of the prestigious award.

Messi stands alone in football history as the only player to achieve the remarkable feat of winning the Ballon d'Or, FIFA World Player of the Year, and UEFA Best Player in Europe Award all in the same year, accomplishing this extraordinary triple crown in both 2011 and 2015.

DID YOU KNOW?

Messi has consistently earned his place among the football elite by being named to the UEFA Team of the Year an astonishing 12 times, spanning from 2008 to 2020.

Messi's supremacy in La Liga has been repeatedly acknowledged, with nine prestigious La Liga Player of the Year awards, recognizing his outstanding performances in the years 2009, 2010, 2011, 2012, 2013, 2015, 2016, 2017, and 2019.

DID YOU KNOW?

Messi's global impact on the sport is exemplified by his five FIFA World Player of the Year titles, earned in 2009, 2010, 2011, 2012, and 2015, making him one of the most celebrated footballers in history.

Messi's exceptional footballing talent has earned him the title of Argentine Footballer of the Year a remarkable 13 times, showcasing his enduring impact on the sport in his home country.

DID YOU KNOW?

Messi had his left foot immortalized in a solid 25-carat gold cast, weighing 55 pounds (25 kilograms) and measuring 10 inches (25.4 centimeters) in height. This golden foot was valued at $5.3 million (£3.4 million) and became a symbol of his footballing prowess. Additionally, a smaller golden footprint was made available for sale at $95,000, and a half-sized gold foot was priced at $42,000. The proceeds from these sales went to the Leo Messi Foundation, supporting those affected by the 2011 tsunami in Japan.

DID YOU KNOW?

Despite his numerous individual football awards and accolades, Lionel Messi has never won the Golden Foot award.

Messi has received three red cards in his illustrious career, with two occurring while representing Argentina and one during his time with FC Barcelona. Despite enduring frequent challenges and fouls on the pitch, Messi's three red cards have made headlines. They are rare occurrences in his otherwise remarkable career.

DID YOU KNOW?

During his youth at Barcelona's La Masia academy, Messi attracted the attention of Arsenal's former manager, Arsene Wenger. Impressed by Messi's potential, Wenger attempted to sign the young talent. However, Messi's status as a budding star within Barcelona's youth ranks was evident, and the Catalan club was determined to retain him. As a result, Messi declined Arsenal's offer and continued his journey with Barcelona.

Messi shares a surprising family connection with his former Barcelona teammate Bojan Krkic. They are fourth cousins, with their family ties tracing back generations. Their common ancestors, Mariano Perez Miralles and Teresa Llobera Minguet, married in Catalonia in 1846. Two family branches emerged from this union: one led by Ramon Perez and the other by Goncal Perez. Ramon's lineage eventually led to Lionel Messi, while Goncal's line produced Bojan Krkic.

DID YOU KNOW?

Messi has been awarded the FIFA World Cup Golden Ball twice in his career. He received this prestigious accolade in the 2014 FIFA World Cup and the 2018 FIFA World Cup.

In an interview with Paris Saint-Germain's official website, he expressed his preference for playing as a second striker, stating, "I've been used to playing in the center, behind the leading striker. It's in this position of the second striker where I feel the most comfortable." He further emphasized his love for being actively involved in the game, adding, "I like to always be in contact with the ball. I like to feel that I am part of the game."

DID YOU KNOW?

Despite being one of the greatest footballers, Lionel is reportedly less skilled at playing FIFA on the PlayStation, as revealed by his former Argentina teammate Pablo Zabaleta. Zabaleta shared that during their time together, he often outplayed Messi, who frequently chose Chelsea as his team in the game. Additionally, Zabaleta humorously noted Messi's lack of culinary skills and modest dancing abilities, painting a picture of a football legend with relatable off-pitch traits.

Messi's iconic goal celebration, where he points toward the sky with both hands after scoring, is a heartfelt tribute to his grandmother, Celia. She was pivotal in sparking Messi's interest in football and supporting his early steps in the sport. Despite her passing in 1998, Messi's touching gesture ensures that her memory and influence remain a significant part of his football journey.

DID YOU KNOW?

As a young football enthusiast, Lionel Messi idolized fellow Argentine and former Valencia and Real Zaragoza playmaker Pablo Aimar. Their paths crossed in La Liga matches, with one memorable encounter in 2004 when Aimar, after a game, offered his shirt to the 17-year-old Messi, who was an unused substitute. Messi cherishes that jersey as a symbol of his admiration. In an interesting turn of events, Aimar later became part of Argentina's 2022 World Cup-winning team, serving as an assistant to head coach Lionel Scaloni.

DID YOU KNOW?

Messi's tattoos are personal works of art that hold deep significance. His left shoulder bears a tattoo of his mother's face, a tribute to her unwavering support. He has inked his firstborn son's name, Thiago, on his calf, symbolizing their strong father-son bond.

Messi has a few well-known superstitions. One of his superstitions is that he enters the field with his right foot first. He also wears the same shin guards his grandmother bought him as a child. Additionally, Messi typically kisses his tattoo of his mother's lips before stepping onto the pitch as a way to pay tribute to her.

DID YOU KNOW?

Messi has surpassed 100 million followers on Instagram, making him one of the few individuals worldwide to achieve this milestone. His Instagram account is a mix of personal moments, football highlights, and endorsements.

Lionel is a well-known pet lover, often sharing his affection for dogs on social media. He has a Dogue de Bordeaux, a breed known for its loyalty and affectionate nature. He frequently posts pictures and videos of his furry companion.

DID YOU KNOW?

Beyond his footballing prowess, Messi showcases his musical talent by playing the guitar during his leisure time. This hobby is a form of relaxation and allows him to unwind from the demands of his high-profile career.

Lionel Messi holds the record for the most appearances on a video game cover by a soccer player, featuring a total of 12 times across the FIFA and eFootball (formerly Pro Evolution Soccer) franchises.

DID YOU KNOW?

From FIFA 06 to FIFA 10, Messi's rating grew from 78 to 90, reflecting his rise from a promising young talent to one of the top players in the game, eventually peaking at 95 by the end of FIFA 10. From FIFA 11 to FIFA 23, Messi consistently held ratings around 90 to 94, showcasing his sustained excellence. He reached multiple 99-rated special cards in FIFA 19 and 20. Despite a gradual decrease in pace, he remained among the top-rated players, with a rating of 91 in FIFA 23, matching other leading players after his move to PSG.

DID YOU KNOW?

Lionel Messi follows a diet focused on hydration and whole foods, including fruits, vegetables, nuts, seeds, and whole grains while avoiding sugar and fried foods. His preferred meal is roasted chicken with root vegetables, providing protein, complex carbs, and vitamins. During training, he limits meat intake, opting for up to three daily protein shakes and plenty of water to aid digestion, stating that excessive meat consumption is challenging for digestion.

Lionel Messi, a native Spanish speaker from Rosario, Argentina, primarily communicates in Spanish. During his over 20-year tenure with FC Barcelona in Spain, he became familiar with the Catalan language, which is prevalent in the region. However, he still needs to acquire proficiency in additional languages, such as English. He has often chosen to express himself in Spanish during public appearances and interviews.

DID YOU KNOW?

Messi follows a structured workout plan to optimize his agility and speed on the field. His regimen includes exercises like lunges, hamstring stretches, and pillar skips for linear speed. For multidirectional speed, he utilizes exercises such as skipping ropes and squats. Messi also works on agility with diagonal hurdles and cone drills, ensuring proper hydration and a cooldown jog to conclude each session.

In a high-profile case, Lionel Messi's 21-month prison sentence for tax fraud was converted into a fine by Spanish courts. He was required to pay €252,000, equivalent to €400 for each day of the original sentence. Messi and his father Jorge were found guilty of defrauding Spain of €4.1m between 2007 and 2009, using tax havens to conceal earnings from image rights. Jorge Messi's 15-month sentence was also replaced with a €180,000 fine.

DID YOU KNOW?

Messi is renowned for wearing the number 10 jersey, a symbol of playmaking excellence, which he donned at FC Barcelona and continues to wear for Argentina. He inherited this iconic number from Ronaldinho in 2008, embodying his role as a leader and one of the greatest players ever. At Paris Saint-Germain, Messi initially wore number 30, his first professional number at Barcelona, before returning to number 10.

Lionel is renowned for his introverted personality, a trait that sets him apart in the typically extroverted world of professional sports. Known for being shy and reserved, especially during his early career, Messi's low-key demeanor is reflected in his modest goal celebrations and his preference for a private life away from the media spotlight. This contrast to the typical image of professional athletes has endeared him to fans who admire his focus on football and personal integrity.

DID YOU KNOW?

Lionel Messi holds an impressive 41 Guinness World Records, with some notable ones being: winning the most Man of the Match awards at the FIFA World Cup with 11, being the first person to assist in five different FIFA World Cups, making the most FIFA World Cup appearances as a captain with 19, and having the most appearances in FIFA World Cup tournaments by a male player, participating in 5 different editions.

Messi's signature move, earning him the nickname "La Pulga" (The Flea), is a testament to his exceptional agility and quickness on the football field. This move involves his ability to change direction rapidly while keeping the ball closely under control, a skill that has become a hallmark of his playing style. His low center of gravity, combined with extraordinary balance and dribbling skills, allows him to navigate through tight spaces and past multiple defenders with ease.

DID YOU KNOW?

Messi has showcased remarkable versatility and evolution in his playing style. Initially famed for his role as a nimble and skillful winger at FC Barcelona, Messi combined his extraordinary dribbling with precise finishing. Gradually, he transitioned into a more central attacking role, often operating as a 'false nine,' where he blended his playmaking abilities with prolific goal-scoring. Later in his career, including his time at Paris Saint-Germain, Messi continued to adapt, taking on more of a creative midfield role while still maintaining his threat in front of goal. Messi has expressed his desire to play football at the highest level into his late 30s, emphasizing his dedication to preserving top physical fitness and performance standards throughout his career.

TRIVIA QUESTIONS!

1) What is Lionel Messi's full name, including his mother's maiden name?
a) Lionel Andrés Messi
b) Lionel Cuccitini Messi
c) Lionel Andrés Messi Cuccitini
d) Lionel Messi Andrés

2) At what age did Lionel Messi start playing soccer?
a) 4
b) 6
c) 8
d) 10

3) Where did Lionel Messi move with his family at the age of 13 to join FC Barcelona's youth academy?
a) Buenos Aires, Argentina
b) Madrid, Spain
c) Rosario, Argentina
d) Barcelona, Spain

4) In which year did Lionel Messi score his first official goal for FC Barcelona?
a) 2003
b) 2004
c) 2005
d) 2006

TRIVIA QUESTIONS!

5) Who did Lionel Messi score his first career hat-trick against in a match that ended in a 3-3 draw?
a) Arsenal
b) Real Madrid
c) Manchester United
d) Chelsea

6) What historic achievement did Argentina's Olympic football team accomplish with Messi's help in 2008?
a) Winning their first gold medal
b) Winning back-to-back Olympic gold medals
c) Winning the FIFA World Cup
d) Winning the Copa América

7) In which year did Lionel Messi win his first Ballon d'Or award?
a) 2007
b) 2008
c) 2009
d) 2010

8) How many Ballon d'Or awards did Lionel Messi win consecutively from 2009?
a) 1
b) 2
c) 3
d) 4

TRIVIA QUESTIONS!

9) At what age did Lionel Messi officially sign his first contract with FC Barcelona?
a) 13
b) 15
c) 17
d) 18

10) Which club did Lionel Messi join after leaving FC Barcelona in 2021?
a) Paris Saint-Germain (PSG)
b) Manchester City
c) Bayern Munich
d) Chelsea

11) How many goals did Messi score in a single UEFA Champions League match against Bayer Leverkusen in 2012?
a) 3
b) 4
c) 5
d) 6

12) What record did Messi break during the 2011-2012 season with Barcelona?
a) Most assists in a season
b) Most goals in a calendar year
c) Most hat-tricks in a season
d) Most free-kick goals in a season

TRIVIA QUESTIONS!

13) At what age did Messi become Barcelona's all-time top scorer in 2012?
a) 22
b) 23
c) 24
d) 25

14) Which award did Messi win in the 2014 FIFA World Cup despite Argentina finishing as runners-up?
a) Golden Boot
b) Golden Glove
c) Golden Ball
d) Best Young Player Award

15) In which year did Messi surpass Telmo Zarra to become the all-time top scorer in La Liga?
a) 2013
b) 2014
c) 2015
d) 2016

16) Messi led Argentina to the Copa América final in 2015. What was the outcome of the final match against Chile?
a) Argentina won in regular time
b) Argentina won on penalties
c) Chile won in regular time
d) Chile won on penalties

TRIVIA QUESTIONS!

17) When did Messi score his 500th goal for Barcelona?
a) 2016
b) 2017
c) 2018
d) 2019

18) What significant achievement did Messi attain in the 2022 FIFA World Cup final?
a) Scored a hat-trick
b) Made his 26th World Cup finals appearance
c) Won the Golden Glove
d) Broke the record for most assists in a World Cup

19) In which year did Lionel Messi marry Antonela Roccuzzo?
a) 2015
b) 2016
c) 2017
d) 2018

20) For which brands has Messi been an endorser?
a) Nike and Coca-Cola
b) Puma and Red Bull
c) Adidas and Pepsi
d) Under Armour and Gatorade

TRIVIA QUESTIONS!

21) What is the name of Lionel Messi's fashion brand?
a) Messi Style
b) The Messi Store
c) Leo's Line
d) Messi Wear

22) What is the name of the restaurant chain owned by Lionel Messi and his family in Argentina?
a) Messi's Cuisine
b) Bellavista del Jardín del Norte
c) Argentine Delights
d) Leo's Eatery

23) What type of cuisine is offered at Bellavista del Jardín del Norte?
a) Spanish
b) Italian
c) Argentine
d) French

24) What is the name of the hotel created by Messi's partnership with the Majestic Hotel Group?
a) Messi's Majestic
b) Majestic Messi
c) Barcelona by Messi
d) Leo's Luxury

TRIVIA QUESTIONS!

25) What type of art does Messi's collection prominently feature?
a) Modernist
b) Surrealist
c) Impressionist
d) Classical

26) What is "The Messi Collection" known for?
a) Sports Equipment
b) Clothing Line
c) Furniture Line
d) Watch Collection

27) How many hat-tricks has Lionel Messi scored in his career?
a) 47
b) 57
c) 67
d) 77

28) What is Messi's record for the fastest hat-trick in La Liga?
a) 10 minutes
b) 12 minutes
c) 15 minutes
d) 18 minutes

TRIVIA QUESTIONS!

29) How many free-kick goals has Messi scored?
a) 55
b) 60
c) 65
d) 70

30) How many head goals has Messi scored?
a) 18
b) 20
c) 23
d) 25

31) How much was Messi's 25-carat gold foot cast valued at?
a) $3.4 million
b) $4.2 million
c) $5.3 million
d) $6.1 million

32) Has Lionel Messi ever won the Golden Foot award?
a) Yes, once
b) Yes, twice
c) No, never
d) No, but he was a finalist

TRIVIA QUESTIONS!

33) How many red cards has Messi received in his career?
a) One
b) Two
c) Three
d) Four

34) Which club did Arsene Wenger try to sign Messi for?
a) Manchester United
b) Arsenal
c) Chelsea
d) Real Madrid

35) How is Messi related to his former teammate Bojan Krkic?
a) Second cousins
b) Third cousins
c) Fourth cousins
d) Not related

36) How many times has Messi won the FIFA World Cup Golden Ball?
a) Once
b) Twice
c) Three times
d) Never

TRIVIA QUESTIONS!

37) What position does Messi prefer to play?
a) Winger
b) Striker
c) Central midfielder
d) Second striker

38) Which team does Messi frequently choose to play in FIFA on PlayStation?
a) Barcelona
b) Manchester City
c) Real Madrid
d) Chelsea

39) Messi's goal celebration, pointing to the sky, is a tribute to whom?
a) His father
b) His grandmother
c) His mother
d) His son

40) Which former Argentine player did Messi idolize?
a) Diego Maradona
b) Gabriel Batistuta
c) Pablo Aimar
d) Juan Román Riquelme

TRIVIA ANSWERS!

1. c) Lionel Andrés Messi Cuccitini
2. a) 4
3. d) Barcelona, Spain
4. c) 2005
5. b) Real Madrid
6. b) Winning back-to-back Olympic gold medals
7. c) 2009
8. d) 4
9. a) 13
10. a) Paris Saint-Germain (PSG)

11. c) 5
12. b) Most goals in a calendar year
13. c) 24
14. c) Golden Ball
15. b) 2014
16. d) Chile won on penalties
17. b) 2017
18. b) Made his 26th World Cup finals appearance
19. c) 2017
20. c) Adidas and Pepsi

TRIVIA ANSWERS!

21. b) The Messi Store
22. b) Bellavista del Jardín del Norte
23. c) Argentine
24. b) Majestic Messi
25. b) Surrealist
26. c) Furniture Line
27. b) 57
28. b) 12 minutes
29. c) 65
30. c) 23

31. c) $5.3 million
32. c) No, never
33. c) Three
34. b) Arsenal
35. c) Fourth cousins
36. b) Twice
37. d) Second striker
38. d) Chelsea
39. b) His grandmother
40. c) Pablo Aimar

SCORE __/40

16-20: Room for Improvement
You're on the right track, but there's more to discover about Messi. Keep learning, and you'll get better!

21-25: Not Bad!
You've got a fair understanding of Lionel Messi. Keep exploring, and you'll improve even more!

26-30: Good Going!
You know quite a bit about Messi. Keep learning, and you'll become an expert in no time!

31-35: Great Job!
You've got a fantastic knowledge of Lionel Messi. Keep up the good work!

36-40: You're a Pro!
Wow, you really know Lionel Messi inside out. You're a true Messi expert!

JOURNAL PAGES

JOURNAL PAGES

JOURNAL PAGES

JOURNAL PAGES

JOURNAL PAGES

WANT A FREE BOOK ON CRISTIANO RONALDO?

Are you ready to delve into the next thrilling book in the series, absolutely free? Get ready to explore the captivating world of yet another football legend!

Just use your smartphone or tablet to scan the QR code below, then follow the simple prompts to receive the PDF.

Made in United States
North Haven, CT
11 December 2023

45605688R00049